WHY MOMMY? MOMMY WHY?

A Children's Book for Parents

By
Joe A. Bass IV

Why Mommy?
Mommy Why?
By Joe A. Bass IV

Published by Clarice Jefferies Publishing
Contact info: cjpublishing@yahoo.com
Copyright © 2024 Joe A. Bass IV

For permissions, contact:
bradley.shanette@yahoo.com

Printed in the United States of America on responsibly sourced paper

I dedicate this book to all parents and grandparents.
As a father who has lost three children, I understand how
love can heal. I think about my angels daily and love them
just as much as my children who are still here.
I pray that you love all children unconditionally, just as God
loves us, and find hope in the enduring nature of love.

"Sunday night, it's time for bed, you have school in the morning," Shami's mommy says. "Prayers and pajamas. Dream bright little light until the sun's rays once again shine bright."

Monday morning, mommy tickles Shami out of a very happy dream,
"Wake up, the sun is up, time to wash your face and brush your teeth."
"Why mommy?" Shami asks.
"Because you want healthy, pretty teeth when you smile and say cheese for your school pictures today."

Mommy lays Shami's clothes on the bed, and Shami gets dressed. "Be sure to put on your jacket, little light," Mommy says. "Why, mommy?" Shami replied. "Because we don't want Jack Frost nipping at your nose, you might catch a cold." Mommy says.

"We're all dressed, we're set, and it's time to go," mommy says as they enter the car. "Put on your seat belt, buckle up tight, little light."
"Why mommy?" Shami asks.
"Because the seat belts will keep us safe whenever mommy drives."

As mommy drives Shami to school, she comes to a stop at the red traffic light.
"Am I at school mommy?" Shami asks.
"No, not yet, little light. Mommy had to stop".
"Why mommy?" Shami asks.
"A red light means stop so other cars can go by," Mommy replies.

Mommy pulls up to the school. "We're here little light, be nice and shine bright. Have a lovely day of learning," says mommy.
"Why mommy?" Shami asks so polite.
"Because you'll shine bright little light if you learn to count, read and write. Now come on, mommy has to get to work. Hugs and Kisses."

Shami hugged and kissed her mother goodbye and was off to class. Due to her inquisitive nature, Shami was a brilliant little girl. She never hesitated to ask questions if there was something she didn't understand.

Shami's mommy was a single parent. She worked hard to be a shining example for Shami. She wanted to show Shami she could do anything she put her mind to.
After a hard day's work, mommy was on her way to pick Shami up from school. While stopped at a red light, a truck hit mommy from behind.
"Oh no!" Mommy says.

The man driving the truck jumped out and rushed to mommy's aide.

"I'm so sorry, ma'am. Are you hurt?" he asked with a panicked urgency.

"No, I'm just a little shaken up," mommy replies.

"I was distracted by my phone," the man says. I am so sorry. Are you sure you are not hurt?"

Frustrated and angry, mommy replies, "I said I'm ok; I just need to pick up my daughter from school."

The man franticly gave mommy a card with his contact information and assured her he'd pay for the damages. Then he jumped in his truck and sped off.

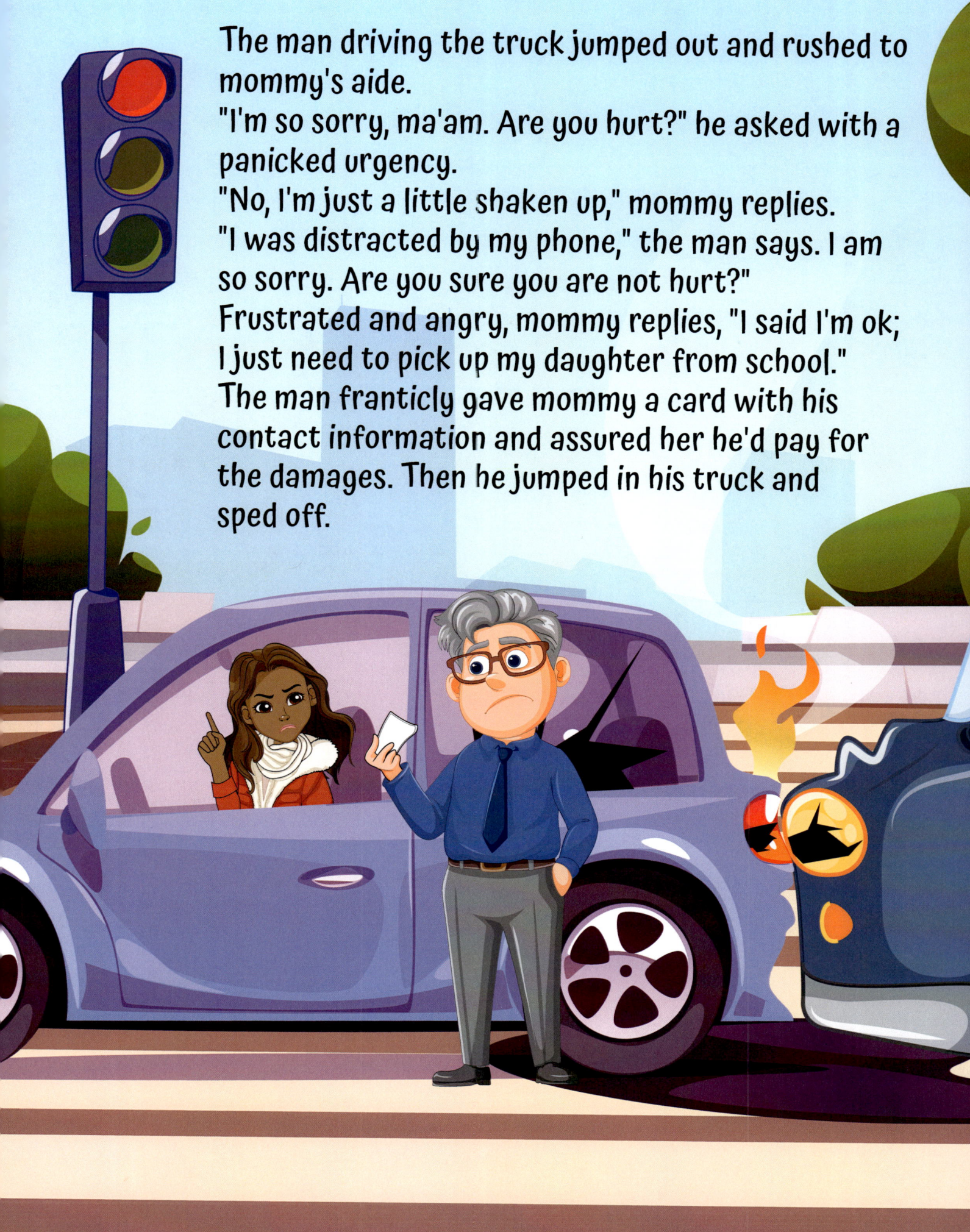

Mommy got back into her car and headed for Shami's school. As she drove, she began to feel a painful, stinging sensation across her chest. She wanted to go to the hospital but thought, "Who's going to pick up Shami from school?"

Fighting through the pain, mommy made it to school. As she approached Shami, she did her very best to appear calm. "Hi, little light," mommy said with a smile, but Shami was not her usual bubbly self. "Hi mommy," Shami sadly replied with her face cast down.

In pain, mommy put Shami into the back seat. Walking around the rear of the car, she noticed the back bumper and trunk were smashed. This upset mommy and added to her pain and frustration.

Mommy tried her best to regain her composure as she entered the car.

"Buckle up, little light," she said as she fastened her seatbelt and adjusted her mirrors.

"Mommy, why..."

Mommy interrupts Shami, "No time for questions; just do it, please."

Mommy never noticed that Shami had already buckled herself in.

1Dyme H

As mommy drove away, the pain in her chest began to intensify. The air through her window caused a cold, wet feeling through her blouse. She reached under her shirt, thinking she was sweating, but to her dismay, she was bleeding. The impact of the accident caused her seatbelt to tighten, thus forcing her nametag to cause a deep cut across her chest.

"Mommy," Shami begins in a somber tone.
"Yes, little light," mommy replies.
"Mommy why..."
Mommy interrupts, "Not now, Shami, please!" Shami quietly removes her seatbelt strap from across her chest and lays on her side across the backseat.

Mommy and Shami arrive at home. Mommy tends to the cut along her chest, and Shami, with her face cast down, slowly walks to her room.

Once mommy finished tending to her injury, she called Shami to the kitchen for a snack. Though Shami was wearing blue pants, mommy noticed a wet stain around the zipper of her jeans.

"Shami, did you have an accident?" Before Shami could respond, mommy said, "Never mind, let's get you in the bath." Mommy begins to draw Shami's bath water.

"Mommy why..."

But again, mommy interrupts, "Not tonight, little light; mommy does not feel good. Just get into the tub, understand?"

"Ok," Shami sadly replies.

Shami sits quietly in the tub while mommy prepares dinner. She does not splash or sing happily as she usually would. "Time for dinner, little light," mommy calls out.

Mommy sets the dinner table and pulls out Shami's favorite seat. Shami does not want to sit down, but fearing she will upset her mother, she says she is not hungry. So, instead, mommy tucks Shami into bed.

"Dream bright, little light, till the rise of the sun shines bright. Don't let the bed bugs bite," mommy says as she tickles Shami. Shami doesn't laugh, not even a smile. Mommy notices that Shami is not her usual self but feels she may have hurt Shami's feelings earlier.
"Don't be upset with mommy little light. I just had a bad day," she says as she kisses Shami goodnight.
"Mommy why..."
"Shhhhh," mommy says, putting her index finger over Shami's lips.
"Well, talk about it in the morning. Get some sleep."

Morning soon came. "Wake up, the sun is up, time to wash your face and brush your teeth," mommy tickled Shami out of her sleep. Shami did not laugh or smile. "C'mon, Little Light, are you still mad at Mommy? You always laugh when I tickle your tummy." Shami quietly walked to the bathroom.

Mommy followed Shami. After Shami was done, she stood up. "You have to clean yourself," mommy says.

"I can't; it hurts," Shami replies.

"Why little light? Why does it hurt?" Shami once again was quiet as she put her head down. With deep concern, mommy placed two fingers under Shami's chin and gently lifted her head. She looked into Shami's eyes and said, "Tell mommy."

"Because of the cleaning man," Shami says.

"What cleaning man, little light?" Mommy asks, her eyes filling with tears.

"The cleaning man that cleans our rest rooms at school," Shami says as she begins to cry.

"What did he do little light?" Mommy asks, trying her best to keep her composure.

"I used the bathroom, and he came in and said he needed to make sure I was clean down there. I'm sorry, mommy," Shami cried, tears streaming down her face.

"No, I'm sorry, little light. I'm so sorry, baby." Mommy cried as she reached for Shami, holding her in her arms and rocking her side to side. "Why didn't you tell me yesterday, little light?" Mommy asks.

"I tried, mommy, but you were mad at me."

"Oh no, baby, I'm sorry, mommy was not mad at you." Shami continued to cry with her face buried in mommy's chest.

As she held Shami, mommy began to reflect on yesterday's events. Shami did try to tell her on several occasions, but it was the way Shami tried to tell her.

Since Shami could speak, she would always ask, **"Why, Mommy?"** But yesterday, every question began, **"Mommy, why?"**

When she picked up Shami from school, she lay in the backseat to avoid sitting on her bottom. There was no water on the bathroom floor from Shami's splashing in the tub, and Shami refused to sit in her favorite seat for dinner, claiming she was not hungry.

Shami would not smile or laugh when tickled; when she woke up this morning, she was not her usual bubbly self. Mommy cried as she held Shami, feeling devasted from missing the warning signs.

Mommy called the school and reported the incident to the principal, who called the authorities. Hours later, they gathered some of the school faculty for a meeting with mommy and Shami. As Shami entered the office, she began to cry.

"What is it, little light?" Mommy asked.

Shami pointed, "That's him," she cried.

Mommy fell to her knees as she cried out... it was the man who rear-ended her car the previous day.

Parents:
Please don't be too busy for your children, they are always "talking" to us.